**In the Name of God the Most
Merciful the Most Compassionate**

بسم الله الرحمن الرحيم

In the Name of God the Most
Merciful the Most Compassionate

THE HEART & THE TONGUE

Their Sicknesses and Cures

**Sheikh
Yassin Roushdy**

DAR AL TAQWA LTD.

© Dar Al Taqwa Ltd. 1999

ISBN 1 870582 21 7

All rights reserved. No part of this publication may be reproduced, stored in a retrieval system, or transmitted, in any form or by any means, electronic, mechanical, photocopying, recording or otherwise, without the prior permission of the publishers.

Edited by Abdalhaqq Bewley and Muhammad Isa Waley

Production: Bookwork, Norwich

Published by:
    Dar Al Taqwa Ltd.
    7A Melcombe Street
    Baker Street
    London NW1 6AE
    email : dar.altaqwa@btinternet.com

Printed and Bound By :
    De-Luxe Printers
    245a Acton Lane
    London NW10 7NR
    website : http://www.de-luxe.com
    email : printers@de-luxe.com

Table of Contents

Introduction — 1

The Importance of Intention — 3

The Sicknesses of the Tongue — 5

  Talking or speaking of what does not concern you — 6
  Showing off and pompousness — 6
  Argumentation — 7
  Shameless language — 8
  Insulting people — 8
  Cursing — 9
  Mockery and derision — 10
  Breaking promises — 10
  Lying — 11
  Backbiting — 13
  Carrying damaging tales — 16
  Praise and commendation — 17

The Sicknesses of the Heart — 19

  Anger — 19
  Envy — 22
  Stinginess — 24
  Ostentation and hypocrisy — 27
  Love of rank, fame and power — 31
  Arrogance — 33

Conclusion — 38

Introduction

The heart is the storehouse of knowledge and wisdom and can guide a person to the noblest knowledge, which is knowledge of Allah. If you know Allah you will do your best to please Him and reach Him. If the heart does not function properly, then it is sick and needs to be treated and cured. Each person, therefore, should search their heart carefully to see what it is filled with: is it occupied with love of Allah or with love of this life and its appetites?

In this context, one must pose an important question: how can the sicknesses of the heart be cured? In answer to this question, there are two steps to follow. Firstly, you should ask Allah to lead you to the Straight Path. In fact, in each prayer when you recite the *Fatiha* and say, *"Guide us on the Straight Path,"* if you say it each time sincerely from the bottom of your heart, Allah will certainly direct you to the Straight Path. Secondly, you must exert yourself to discover the sicknesses of your heart and to cure them by keeping away from all the sins or prohibited deeds which fill your heart with impurities.

The purpose of this set of discourses is to shed light on some of the most serious illnesses of the tongue and heart which many of us neglect since we are not aware of their gravity. The role of intention as a prime factor in one's deeds will be a recurrent theme throughout these lessons.

The Importance of Intention

There are four stages that a person goes through before committing a sin. In the first stage the idea crosses their mind – and in most cases it is Shaytan who insinuates this idea into the mind. You are not condemned at this stage, because you cannot control or stop Shaytan from inspiring you. In the second stage you feel the desire to do the action. For example, a person is fasting and while he is walking in the street he smells a certain kind of food that he loves and automatically feels the pangs of hunger and the desire to eat it. This is a feeling which you cannot control and hence you are not punished for it.

In the third stage you become inclined to commit the sin. In the fourth stage you intend to commit the sin: you have made up your mind. At this stage you are judged by Allah as the Prophet, may Allah bless him and grant him peace, said, "Actions are only judged according to intentions."

In fact, intentions are very important as they are the sole determinant of the worth of one's deeds. The same act can be considered a good deed or a sin depending on the intention of the doer. Let us give a few examples to clarify this.

- A man leaves his house with the intention of killing another person. He waits for him and then shoots at him. Even if it transpires that he misses his target and the person is unharmed, the man is still considered a killer since his intention was to kill.

- If, before going to sleep, a man decides to commit a certain sin in the morning but then dies before the morning comes, he will be judged for that sin. Therefore you must be very careful, keep your intentions pure, and never decide to do anything sinful.

- A married man agrees with his mistress to go to a house to spend some time with her in order to commit adultery. Before leaving his house, he realises that he is about to do something sinful and that Allah will punish him for that, so he changes his mind and asks Allah for forgiveness. In that case he will be rewarded, as the following *hadith qudsi* says: "Whoever intends to do an evil action and then does not do it, Allah will record a full good action for him." (Bukhari and Muslim)

- Take the same example, but this time the man goes to his mistress's house. Just before going up to her apartment he sees her husband coming, so he leaves in a hurry before her husband can notice him. In this case, although he has not committed adultery he will be judged for it because what stopped him from committing the sin was an external factor and not fear of Allah.

In fact, if you think about repenting of a sin, you will find that repentance comes in different degrees. The highest degree is when you repent immediately after the thought of committing the sin comes to your mind. The Qur'an refers to believers of that kind in *al-A'raf* (7:201): *"As for those who are godfearing, when they are troubled by a visitation from Shaytan, they remember and immediately see clearly."* The second degree is when you repent after you have made up your mind to commit the sin, as in the example we gave. The third level is to repent after actually committing the sin, and that is the lowest degree.

The Sicknesses of the Tongue

The tongue is one of the organs of the body which can either elevate the status of the individual or drive him to the depths of ignominy. The Prophet, may Allah bless him and grant him peace, said, "A man is judged by his smallest organs: his heart and his tongue." The Prophet also said, "Whoever believes in Allah and the Last Day should speak good words or be silent." *(Riyad as-Salihin*, no. 1511)

Sufyan ibn 'Abdullah relates: "I said, 'Messenger of Allah, tell me something which I can cling to.' He replied, 'Say "My Lord is Allah" and then go straight.' I asked, 'Messenger of Allah, what is the thing which you fear most for me?' The Prophet, may Allah bless him and grant him peace, took hold of his tongue and then said, 'This.'" *(Riyad as-Salihin*, no. 1517.)

Allah says in the Qur'an: *"Do you do not see how Allah makes a likeness of a good word: a good tree whose roots are firm and whose branches are in heaven?"* (Ibrahim 14:24) This verse shows the importance of uttering good words and the reward one gets by uttering only good words.

Allah also says in the Qur'an: *"He does not utter a single word, without a watcher by him, pen in hand."* (*Qaf* 50:18) This verse emphasises that every word you say is recorded, and hence on the Day of Judgement it will be found written down in the record of your deeds. All these Qur'anic verses and *hadiths* show how important it is to take the utmost care of what you say. In the following section a brief discussion of some of the important illnesses of the tongue will be presented.

Talking or speaking of what does not concern you

The Prophet, may Allah bless him and grant him peace, once visited Ka'b, one of his Companions, when he was ill. When he saw Ka'b, he said to him, "Good news, Ka'b!" When Ka'b's mother heard the Prophet say that, she said, "Congratulations, Ka'b, on Paradise." She thought that by "good news" the Prophet meant that Ka'b would enter Paradise. The Prophet told her, "How do you know, mother of Ka'b, that your son will enter Paradise? Perhaps he talked about matters that did not concern him, or withheld something that he owed!"

This implies that if someone frequently talks about matters which do not concern him, this may keep him away from Paradise. This is because it usually leads to more serious sins such as backbiting or suspicion. Here is an example. A man is walking with a friend when he sees another friend passing by in a car. He asks his friend, "Isn't that 'Ali?" His friend answers, "Yes, I believe so." The man says, "Who is that woman sitting beside him in the car?" His friend replies, "I do not know. I have never seen her before." The man goes on, "But he is not married, so who is the woman?" and so on. In this way many sins are committed; the starting point is asking about something which does not concern the two people involved.

Showing off and pompousness

This happens when you aim at finding mistakes in the speech of another person regarding the wording, meaning, or objective of the speaker. For example, when you are in a meeting and your boss starts speaking, you might say to your colleague, "Did you hear that? He does not know how to express himself. What he is saying is illogical and he is making a lot of grammatical mistakes." In this case you are picking out whatever is wrong with his speech and exposing it to others.

Another example: you are sitting in the mosque and someone stands up and starts urging people to contribute to building a hospital. You say to your friend, "This person is just showing off. He wants to prove that he is a good Muslim." You have therefore questioned the intention or motive of this person.

If you are listening to someone speaking and what he is saying is wrong, then if the matter is not important or not related to religion, it is recommended to keep quiet and not to correct him – or, if you do correct him, to do it secretly and not openly in order not to embarrass him.

Argumentation

The type of arguing referred to here is that which has as its objective to show yourself as the one who is right, the one who knows better, and not merely to reveal the truth. Suppose you are sitting in a meeting or lecture and the speaker conveys a false piece of information; ask yourself this question, "Would I be equally satisfied if someone else corrected the speaker or do I want to be the one who corrects him?" If you are equally satisfied, then you are not the type of person referred to here, If, however, you want to be the one who corrects the speaker, this is dangerous because in that case your motive is not to reveal the truth but to have the truth revealed by you.

There is a very meaningful story which teaches us how to correct someone else in a courteous way and without hurting them. The two grandsons of the Prophet, may Allah bless him and grant him peace, al-Hasan and al-Husayn, once saw an old man performing ablution in an incorrect manner and wanted to inform him about this in a courteous way. They went to him and asked him, "Please, brother in Islam, would you to be the judge between us because we differ in opinion as to how to make ablution? Would you be kind enough to observe us and then tell us who is right?" The man agreed and they started performing *wudu'* in front of him, When they finished, he told them, "You are both right. It is I who make mistakes in my ablution. No wonder that wisdom comes from you, grandsons of the Prophet!"

Shameless language

Shameless language (*al-fuhsh*) means expressing ugly matters explicitly and openly. In Islam it is recommended to use metaphors rather than to talk about ugly things explicitly. If we read the Qur'an carefully, we will learn how and when to use these metaphors. In *Surat al-A'raf* (7:189) Allah says: *"Then when he covered her she bore a light load and carried on with it."* When Allah wants to allude to sexual intercourse between husband and wife, He says: *"Then when he covered her."* When He wants to mention the process of answering the call of nature, He says in *Surat an-Nisa'* (4:43): *"If you are ill or on a journey, or any of you have come a low place."* One word in Arabic for 'lavatory' is *'al-gha'it'* which means a low place. At that time, in the absence of water closets, whenever someone wanted to ease themselves, they would go apart to a low place in order not to be seen. The Qur'an therefore referred to the process itself by mentioning the place where it is done. The rest of the verse says, *"if you have touched women."* Here again a euphemism is used to refer to sexual intercourse.

Insulting People

Surat al-Hujurat (49:11) prohibits insults: *"O you who believe! People should not ridicule others who may well be better than themselves; nor should any women ridicule other women who may well be better than themselves. And do not find fault with one another or insult each other with derogatory nicknames."*

The Prophet, may Allah bless him and grant him peace, said, "It is a great sin for someone to insult his parents. He was asked, "How could someone insult their own parents, Messenger of Allah?" The Prophet answered, "A man insults another man's parents and so the other answers him back by insulting his parents."

Cursing

Cursing means asking for someone to be kept away from Allah and to be deprived of His Mercy. Cursing is mentioned in the Qur'an where Allah curses Shaytan who refused to obey Allah and bow to Adam. A number of *hadiths* prohibit cursing. The Prophet, may Allah bless him and grant him peace, said, "Do not curse one another with Allah's curse or His anger or Hellfire." (*Riyad as-Salihin*, no. 1554) He also said, "When a person curses something, the curse rises to the heaven and the gates of heaven are locked against it. Then it falls to earth and the gates of the earth are locked against it, and then it goes to the right and to the left and when it does not find any entrance, it returns to what was cursed if it deserves it. If not, it returns to the one who spoke it." (*Riyad as-Salihin*, no. 1556)

This last *hadith* shows how dangerous cursing is because if you curse something or someone who does not deserve to be cursed, the curse will rebound on you. The Prophet was also reported as saying, "A man does not accuse another man of iniquity or disbelief without that rebounding onto him if the other man does not have what is imputed to him." (*Riyad as-Salihin*, no. 1560)

This means that we are not allowed to curse anybody except those who have been cursed in the Qur'an, such as Shaytan, the unbelievers in general – not a specific unbeliever – and oppressors in general. Only those three and the Pharaohs of Egypt were cursed by Allah in the Qur'an. If you know an unbeliever, are you allowed to curse him? The answer is no, because that unbeliever might embrace Islam before he dies.

Allah says: *"Allah does not like evil words to be voiced out loud, except in the case of someone who has been wronged. Allah is All-Hearing, All-Knowing."* (4:148) According to this verse you are not allowed to say any bad words in public or in front of anyone except on one condition – "in the case of someone who has been wronged" – and even then, what you are permitted to say is only the details of your case without insulting or cursing. The rest of the verse says, "Allah is All-Hearing, All-Knowing": Allah hears you and knows that you were subject to injustice, and He alone can help you.

When the Prophet Nuh, may Allah bless him and grant him peace, suffered from the persecution of his people who refused to believe him, made fun of him, and accused him of being mad: *"He called upon his Lord, 'I am overwhelmed, so help me!'"* (54:10) He did not insult his people or ask Allah to punish them. He only said, "I am overwhelmed, so please, Allah, help me." This is an example of how a good Muslim should behave.

Mockery and derision

Allah says: *"O you who believe, people should not ridicule others who may well be better than themselves. Nor should any women ridicule other women who may well be better than themselves. And do not find fault with one another or insult each other with derogatory nicknames."* (49:11)

According to this verse you should not laugh at other people, since it may well be that they are better than you. In fact, even if you really are better than the person you are making fun of, by mocking him you lower your status and hence he becomes better than you. If you are laughing at someone because of some physical attribute, such as being black or ugly or disabled, then you are actually making fun of Allah – for it is Allah who created him this way.

The Prophet, may Allah bless him and grant him peace, said, "Whoever makes fun of his brother because of a sin of which he has already repented, will surely commit the same sin during his life." (Narrated by at-Tirmidhi)

Breaking Promises

Allah says: *"O you who believe, fulfil your contracts!"* (5:1) The Prophet also said, may Allah bless him and grant him peace, "There are three signs of a hypocrite: when he speaks he lies;

when he makes a promise, he breaks it; and when he is trusted, he betrays his trust." (*Riyad as-Salihin*, no. 199, Bukhari and Muslim)

Since breaking a promise is considered a sin, you must try not to make a promise unless it is necessary to do so. Moreover, you should always, when making a promise, add the word *"insha' Allah"* (if Allah wills), so that Allah may help you to fulfil it. You should remember that if you make a promise while intending to break it you are a hypocrite. For example, if someone asks you to find a job for his son and you promise him to do your best while you intend to do nothing about it, then you are a hypocrite, and hypocrisy is not the attribute of a believer.

Lying

The Prophet, may Allah bless him and grant him peace, said, "Truthfulness leads to piety, and piety leads to Paradise. A person should be truthful until he is written down as truthful in the sight of Allah. Lying leads to deviance, and deviance leads to the Fire. A person lies to the point that he is written down as a liar in the sight of Allah."(*Riyad as-Salihin*, no. 54) There are different degrees and types of falsehoods as explained in the following *hadiths*:

> The Prophet, may Allah bless him and grant him peace, said, "Anyone who relates a dream which he has not really had will have to tie a knot between two grains of barley and will not be able to do it." (*Riyad as-Salihin*, no. 1544)
>
> He said, may Allah bless him and grant him peace, "The worst of lies is when a man says his eyes have seen something which they have not seen."(*Riyad as-Salihin*, no. 1545)
>
> A woman came to the Allah and asked, "Messenger of Allah, I have a co-wife. Would it be a sin if I were to pretend to have received something from my husband which he has not given me?" The Prophet replied, "Anyone who pretends to have re-

ceived something he has not been given is like someone who wears two spurious garments." (*Riyad as-Salihin*, no. 1549)

The Prophet, may Allah bless him and grant him peace, was once visiting a family in Madina. He heard the mother calling her son and telling him, "Come here, son, and I will give you something sweet." The Prophet asked her, "Are you really going to give him something?" She replied, "Yes, I am going to give him some dates." The Prophet told her, "I swear by Allah that if you were not intending to give him anything it would have been considered a lie." (Abu Dawud)

Al-Bukhari, the most famous collector of authenticated *hadiths* of the Prophet, once travelled to visit a man who was noted for his knowledge of *hadiths*. While he was sitting with him, the man's camel ran away. He went after it and pretended that he was going to offer it some food. When al-Bukhari saw this he left. The man came running after him and asked him why he had left. Al-Bukhari told him, "I would not take a *hadith* of the Prophet from a man who lied to a camel."

Although falsehood is basically unlawful or *haram*, in exceptional cases it can be permissible. If telling a lie may be the means to achieve a lawful object but this object could also be achieved without resort to lying, then it is unlawful to tell a lie. If a commendable object cannot be achieved without resort to lying, lying may be permissible. If the achievement of an object is lawful and permitted by *Shari'a*, then lying to achieve it is also permissible while if the achievement of this object is obligatory, it becomes obligatory to lie to achieve the said goal.

For example, if a Muslim has hidden himself from fear of some tyrant and you are asked about him, you should lie. Similarly, if somebody holds another person's property on trust and a tyrannical person is after it, then in order to protect it the custodian of the property must lie. In that case the best course for him is to employ *'tawriya'* while speaking to the tyrant. *'Tawriya'* means that while speaking, the speaker should tell the truth, but in such terms as to lead the listener astray. If he does not employ *'tawriya'* or indirect hints but tells a direct lie, then this is also lawful.

In this connection a tradition of the Prophet, may Allah bless him and grant him peace, is quoted by al-Bukhari and Muslim from Umm Kulthum. She said that she heard the Prophet say that someone who employs good words to make peace between people is not a liar. In his version, Muslim added the following words: "Umm Kulthum said, 'I did not hear him make an allowance regarding anything that people say except in three cases: in war, putting things right between people, and what a man says to his wife and a wife says to her husband." (*Riyad as-Salihin*, chap. 261)

Backbiting

Allah says: *"O you who believe, avoid most suspicion. Indeed some suspicion is a crime. And do not spy and do not backbite one another. Would any of you like to eat his brother's dead flesh?"* (49:12) The Prophet, may Allah bless him and grant him peace, defined the meaning of backbiting for his Companions in a *hadith* related in *Sahih Muslim*. He asked the Companions, "Do you know what is meant by backbiting?" They said, "Allah and His Messenger know best." He said, "To mention your brother in a manner he dislikes." It was said, "What if my brother is as I say?" He replied, "If he is as you said, then you are guilty of backbiting him. If he is not as you said, you have slandered him." (*Riyad as-Salihin*, no. 1523)

Committing slander is mentioned in the Qur'an: *"And those who abuse believing men and women, without their having justly merited it, bear the weight of slander and clear wrongdoing."* (33:58) This verse refers to those who wrongly accuse men and women of sins they have not committed or attributes they do not have. Committing slander, therefore, is different from backbiting.

A third category is *'ifk'*, which means to pass on rumours whether true or not. *'Ifk'* is referred to in the Qur'an: *"You were bandying it about on your tongues, your mouths uttering something about which you had no knowledge. You considered it a trivial matter, but in Allah's sight it is an enormity."* (24:15) So if you hear something bad about someone and you go around repeating what you heard, this is *'ifk'*.

Backbiting may be the result of anger or envy, the desire to make fun of people, showing yourself as better than others, trying to be in agreement with the group you are socialising with, or passing the time discussing the behaviour of others. An important point to take note of is that backbiting can be disguised as a virtuous deed. For example, you can pretend that you are enjoining virtue or forbidding evil by saying, "This man does not pray. This is not right. A good Muslim should not do that." If your intention to enjoin virtue is really sincere you should advise the person in secret instead of advising him in public.

Backbiting can also be disguised under the cloak of showing mercy to someone. For example, you might say to your friends, "This person prays and fasts, but he drinks alcohol; let's pray that Allah guides him to the right path." If you are really sincere, you should pray for him in secret instead of exposing his sins in public. Backbiting can take the form of words, behaviour, mimicry, sarcasm or insult. Allah says: *"Woe to every faultfinding backbiter."* (104:1) It is also possible to backbite someone without mentioning his name but instead by referring to one of his attributes that is well-known to those who listen to you.

What makes backbiting a very dangerous sin is that repentance is not enough to absolve you from it. The person you spoke about must forgive you first. If he does not, then on the Day of Judgement he will take from your good deeds or you will take on some of his sins. It is related that al-Hasan, the grandson of the Prophet, was informed that someone had backbitten him. He therefore asked his servant to take some fruits and go to that person with a letter in which he wrote, "I was told that you had given me some of your good deeds as a present. I will not be able to do the same, so please accept these fruits as a gift from me."

To keep away from backbiting, therefore, you should first remind yourself that if you commit this sin, on the Day of Judgement the person you have backbitten will take from your good deeds or give you some of his sins. Secondly, remember that you should keep yourself busy with your own faults and flaws instead of searching for other people's. Thirdly, try to find out your reasons for backbiting. Are you motivated by a feeling of anger towards the person you backbite? If so, why do you not forgive this person instead and be among the followers of the following verse? *"They should rather pardon and overlook. Would you not love Allah to forgive you?"* (24:22)

If you are sitting in a group of people and they start backbiting someone and you join them to please them, remember that if you please people at the cost of displeasing Allah, Allah will be displeased with you and will make people dissatisfied with you as well. So if you find yourself in such a group you should defend the person who is being backbitten; if you cannot, try to change the topic of conversation or else leave the place. If you cannot leave, then in your heart you should object to what is being said.

Backbiting is a sickness of the tongue and of the heart as well, because it is possible to backbite without uttering a single word. For example, if you are talking to yourself and you mention something bad about someone, this is considered backbiting and it enters the realm of suspicion. Allah says: *"O you who believe, avoid most suspicion. Indeed some suspicion is a crime."* (49:12) Suspicion tends to impel you to spy in order to find out whether your suspicions are correct or not. That is the reason why the previous verse continues as follows: *"And do not spy, and do not backbite one another."*

Backbiting, therefore, constitutes a series of sins, each leading to the next. First you suspect, then you spy on the person, and eventually you start backbiting him in public.

There are, however, circumstances in which it is permissible to speak about people for religious purposes when it is indispensable to do so. This can apply in six instances.

- A report for the redress of some injustice, wrong, tyranny or high-handedness. In such case an oppressed person can petition the ruler, judge, or somebody in authority, against a person who has perpetrated such an injustice.
- When seeking help to stop some practice or action which may

be against the principles of religion.

- When seeking religious advice (*fatwa*) on some specific topic from a qualified person.

- If somebody openly indulges in evil practices such as drinking liquor or usurping people's property.

- To caution Muslims about the evil consequences of some mischief.

- To introduce somebody when such person is already known with by a nickname such as 'deaf', 'blind', or 'squint-eyed'. In such a case his introduction with by a nickname is permissible. But to use such words to humiliate or make fun of him is forbidden.

Carrying damaging tales

Allah says: *"But do not obey any vile swearer of oaths, any backbiter, slander-monger."* (68:10-11) The Prophet, may Allah bless him and grant him peace, said, "A slanderer will not enter the Garden." (*Riyad as-Salihin*, no. 1536) He also said, while passing by two graves, "They are being punished, and not for anything very great. One of them did not guard himself from urine and the other was involved in backbiting." (*Riyad as-Salihin*, no. 1537)

According to the *hadiths*, although many people are not aware that carrying tales is a prohibited deed, it is considered a very serious sin which a good Muslim should keep away from. If someone comes to you and tells you that another person has criticised you, that is tale-bearing. You should not believe what you are told, and you should correct the person who carried the tale to you and advise them not to repeat it. You should be careful not to be motivated by what you have heard and you must not let it lead you to commit sins such as spying on that person to find out whether he really criticised you or not.

If you see someone committing a sin that affects other people, such as theft, then you should expose him and report what you saw to the authorities, but your intention should be the benefit of the community and not personal revenge. If, however, this sin is individual, such as private drinking, you should not go around relating what you witnessed to people.

A man once came to 'Umar ibn 'Abdu'l-'Aziz – the fifth rightly-guided caliph, who was known for his great justice – and warned him against a certain person who had criticised him. Upon hearing this, 'Umar told the man, "If you are lying, then you are the subject of the verse that says, *'O you who believe, if a degenerate person brings you a report, scrutinise it carefully lest you attack people in ignorance...* (49:6), and therefore you are to be considered degenerate. If, on the other hand, you are telling the truth, then are the subject the verse that says, *'a backbiter, slandermonger,'* (68:11) and you will be despised for that. But if you wish to repent, we will forgive you." The man asked for forgiveness.

Praising and commendation

Some types of commendation or praise also are not permissible, such as attributing to someone qualities of which only Allah can know. For example, if you say, "This person is really pious: he is a true believer," you have commended him with an attribute which Allah alone knows. You can never be sure whether a person is pious or not. The Prophet, may Allah bless him and grant him peace, advised his Companions when they praised anyone to add the words, "I think". For example, "I think 'Ali is pious."

If you want to praise someone, praise him with qualities which you can know he has, such as saying, "'Ali prays regularly in the mosque." This is accepted because you see him praying every day in the mosque. But it is not permissible to say, "This person's prayers are accepted by Allah."

If you are the one who is being praised, be careful not to become arrogant or satisfied with yourself, for that might make you exert less effort than before to please Allah. There is a supplication which the Prophet, may Allah bless him and grant him peace, taught Abu Bakr to say when he was praised: "O Allah, forgive me for the sins they do not know, do not condemn me for what they say, and make me better than they think."

The Prophet, may Allah bless him and grant him peace, praised many of his Companions. He said, "If there were to be another prophet after me, it would be 'Umar ibn al-Khattab." He also said, "If one were to weigh the faith of Abu Bakr and that of the rest of the world, Abu Bakr's faith would be weightier." He also said, "I am the city of knowledge and 'Ali ibn Abi Talib is its gate." When the Prophet, may Allah bless him and grant him peace, praised his Companions, he praised them truthfully and sincerely and was well aware of their attributes. As for the Companions themselves, they were very fearful of Allah and very modest and were therefore above arrogance.

It is related that when 'Umar ibn al-Khattab was lying down dying after having been stabbed in the back by a slave he told his son, "Remove the pillow from under my head and put my head on the sand - perhaps Allah will forgive me!"

The Sicknesses of the Heart

We have looked at several of the ways in which our tongues can betray us and how these verbal sicknesses can be cured. Yet the tongue can never be more than the interpreter of what lies in the heart, and in the end it is the heart which is the most important factor in the eventual destiny of every human being – dictating whether we will be inhabitants of Paradise or of Hellfire.

Allah says in *Surat ash-Shu'ara* when speaking of the people who will enter Paradise: *"...except to those who bring to Allah sound hearts."* (26:87) And in a famous *hadith* the Prophet made this matter very clear to us: "There is a lump of flesh in the body, the nature of which is that when it is sound, the entire body is sound, and when it is corrupt, the entire body is corrupt: it is the heart." (*Riyad as-Salihin* no. 588)

From this it is clear that the health of the heart is of paramount importance to every human being and so it is essential for us to examine the major sicknesses of the heart and the way they can be cured. So in this section we will look at anger, envy, stinginess, hypocrisy, love of power, and arrogance.

Anger

A minimum level of anger is a necessary attribute for every human being to enable us to protect ourselves and what belongs to us. Anger should, however, be moderate and not excessive so that it does not to lead to unpleasant consequences. Moderate anger means that you should be angry regarding things that are considered to be necessities or related to religion.

This moderation in anger is achieved by removing from the heart love for and attachment to unnecessary things. You should keep in mind that whatever happens is Allah's will. Suppose, for example, you wanted to get a certain job but you were not accepted; you get angry and upset because you did not achieve your aim. You should think of it this way: what has happened can only be Allah's will and it is clearly nonsensical to put your own will or desire above that of Allah.

According to several *hadiths* related by at-Tirmidhi and al-Bayhaqi, the Prophet, may Allah bless him and grant him peace, said that when a Muslim feels angry, he should do the following. If he is standing, he should sit down. If he is sitting down, he should lie down. If he is lying down, he should go and make ablution or have a bath. This is because when you get angry you tend to move forward. If you are sitting, you tend to stand up. Hence by doing the reverse you can control or curb your anger.

Allah says: *"Race each other to forgiveness from your Lord and a Garden whose breadth is the heavens and the earth, prepared for the godfearing: those who give in times of both ease and hardship, those who control their rage and pardon other people. Allah loves those who do good."* (3:133-134)

The Prophet, may Allah bless him and grant him peace, said, "If someone restrains his anger when he is able to give vent to it, Allah – glory be to Him and may He be exalted – will summon him at the head of all creatures on the Day of Resurrection so that he may chose whichever of the wide-eyed houris he wishes." (*Riyad as-Salihin*, no. 47; related by al-Bukhari) A man asked the Prophet, may Allah bless him and grant him peace, to give him counsel. He said, "Do not get angry." He repeated his request several times and every time he said, "Do not get angry." (*Riyad as-Salihin*, no. 48; related by al-Bukhari)

It is related that 'Umar ibn al-Khattab was walking one day when a drunk man appeared before him. 'Umar ordered that the man should be beaten for being drunk. When he did so, the man insulted him. 'Umar, upon hearing the man insulting him, ordered the people to stop beating him. When he was asked why, he said, "Because if I now order you to beat him, the anger will be for myself and not for the sake of Allah, and hence I might punish him excessively."

It is also related that 'Ali ibn Abi Talib, the Prophet's cousin and the husband of his daughter Fatima, was fighting in a battle and was on the point of striking one of the unbelievers with his sword. The unbeliever spat in his face and when he did so, 'Ali put down his sword and did not kill him. When he was asked the reason for this, he said, "If I kill him now, it will be because he spat on me and not for the sake of Allah (i.e. out of anger on his own account and not from anger for the sake of Allah)."

If we go back to the *ayat* in *Surat Ali 'Imran*, *"Race each other to forgiveness from your Lord and a Garden whose width is the heavens and the earth, prepared for the godfearing: those who give in times of both ease and hardship, those who control their rage and pardon other people. Allah loves good-doers,"* (3:133-134) we find that the reward of suppressing anger and forgiving people who harm one is immense: a Garden whose width is that of the heavens and of the earth.

The Prophet, may Allah bless him and grant him peace, said, "*Sadaqa* does not decrease wealth in any way: for pardoning someone Allah only increases a person in might, and no one is humble without Allah Almighty elevating him." (*Riyad as-Salihin*, no. 556)

It is also related that 'Ali ibn Abi Talib once ordered his slave girl to bring him warm water to wash with. She brought him very hot water and when she poured it on his hands it hurt him badly. She noticed that he became very angry and said to him, "O Comman-der of the Believers, remember the verse in the Qur'an which says, *'those who control their rage'*," so he said, "I forgive you." She added, *"Allah loves good-doers."* He replied, "Go, you are no longer a slave. You are free."

When Abu Bakr wanted to withhold his charity from one of his relatives who had slandered and gossiped maliciously about his daughter 'A'isha, the following verse was revealed to the Prophet: *"Those of you possessing affluence and ample wealth should not make oaths that they will not give to their relatives and the very poor and those who have emigrated for the Cause of Allah. They should rather pardon and overlook. Would you not love Allah to forgive you? Allah is Ever-Forgiving, Most Merciful."* (24:22) When Abu Bakr heard this verse, he wept and said, "Of course I would love Allah to forgive me," and he resumed the payment of charity to his relative.

We learn from this verse that we should not let anger keep us away from giving people their rights or giving them what we used to give. A more rewarding deed would be to give them more than their rights even though they have caused us harm.

It is related that the Prophet, may Allah bless him and grant him peace, was once sitting with Abu Bakr when a man came and started insulting Abu Bakr. Abu Bakr kept silent until he could no longer be patient and answered the man back. When he did so, the Prophet left. Abu Bakr asked the Prophet, "Messenger of Allah! He insulted me and you kept silent, but when I started to answer back you left." The Prophet said. "Abu Bakr, while you were silent the angels answered for you but when you started answering the man the angels left and Shaytan came. I would not sit in the same place as Shaytan."

Envy

The Prophet, may Allah bless him and grant him peace, said: "Beware of envy. Envy devours good actions as fire devours kindling wood." (*Riyad as-Salihin*, no. 1569)

Envy can take various different forms:

- Wishing that a person who enjoys a blessing will lose it.
- Wishing to have the same blessing and for the other person to lose it.
- You wish to have the same blessing, and if you cannot have it you wish that the other person would lose it.
- You wish to have the same blessing, without hoping that the other person loses it.

This last type of envy is permissible as long as the blessing you wish to obtain is lawful.

Several examples of envy are cited in the Qur'an, such as the story of the Prophet Yusuf who was envied by his own brothers on account of his father's love for him. Their envy induced them to throw him in a well to get rid of him and to lie to their father, pretending that a wolf had eaten him. (*Surat Yusuf*, 12)

As for envy concerning non-worldly matters – rivalry in matters related to religion – this type of envy has a better connotation in Arabic and is permissible as the Prophet, may Allah bless him and grant him peace, said: "You may only have envy in two ways: a man to whom Allah has given wealth which he spends for the truth; and a man to whom Allah has given wisdom and who acts by it and teaches it." (*Riyad as-Salihin*, no. 1569)

Let us give an example to illustrate this point. Suppose you see a very wealthy man who spends for the Cause of Allah. You pray for him and ask Allah to bless him and give him even more money. You also ask Allah to provide you with equal wealth so that you may be able to spend on the poor and needy and help in preaching for and calling people to Islam. If Allah does not provide you with the wealth you have asked for, He will give you a reward equal to that of this rich man because people are judged according to their intentions.

Ibn Sirin, a well-known religious scholar, said, "I never envied anyone for a blessing in this world. If he is going to Paradise, why should I envy him for this life which is very trivial compared to Paradise? And if he is going to Hell, why should I envy him for this life when punishment is awaiting him? I should rather feel sorry for him. So in neither case is it sensible to envy him."

Anas ibn Malik related: "We were sitting with the Prophet, may Allah bless him and grant him peace, when he said, 'You will now see a man who will enter Paradise;' and we saw a man of the Ansar. The next day the Prophet said the same thing and we saw the same man. 'Abdullah ibn al-'As wanted to find out what extra acts of worship this man performed for him to deserve Paradise. He followed the man to his house and asked him to give him hospitality for three nights. The man welcomed him and 'Abdullah started to observe the man's behaviour. He found that he was performing no extra acts of worship (no additional prayers or fasting), except that when he woke up from sleep he would invoke Allah. 'Abdullah was puzzled and told the man of the real reason behind his visit. The man said, 'I only do what you have seen – but I swear by Allah that I have never cheated a Muslim or envied him for any blessing he possesses.' When he heard this, 'Abdullah said, 'This is the quality which most of us lack and which has made you one of the people of Paradise.'"

Stinginess

The Prophet, may Allah bless him and grant him peace, said: "Stinginess and bad conduct are not attributes of a true believer." Allah says: *"Allah does not love anyone vain and boastful. As for those who are stingy and command other people to stinginess, and hide the bounty Allah has given them..."* (4:36-37) The main reason for stinginess is love of wealth, which has four main causes:

- You love wealth because it is a means to acquire worldly things.
- You accumulate wealth because you think that your life will extend long enough to allow you to enjoy it.
- You accumulate wealth for your children to secure their needs after your death.
- You do not trust for the future and hence you try to accumulate as much wealth as possible now.

Stinginess is a very common human character flaw and many of us need to know how to combat it in ourselves. Each of the above causes of stinginess must be examined separately so that we may be able to deal with it effectively.

- Those who accumulate wealth as a means of acquiring worldly benefits should make sure to spend it on lawful things. They should also be content, pay their *zakat* readily and willingly, give charity and spend much for the Cause of Allah.

- Those who think that life will be long enough for them to enjoy what they have accumulated should remind themselves of the Day of Judgement and that life is short and death imminent. 'Abdullah ibn Shikhkhir said, "I presented myself before the Prophet, may Allah bless him and grant him peace, while he was reciting *Surat at-Takathur* (102): *"Fierce competition for this world has distracted you..."* He added, "Man says, 'My property, my property!' But o Son of Adam, what do you gain from your property except for what you have eaten which has vanished, what you have dressed in which has become worn out, and what you have spent in charity and therefore sent ahead (to the Next World)?"

- If you accumulate wealth for your children, you should remember the verse: *"People should show concern for them in the same way that those who were leaving small children behind would feel fear on their account. They should show fear of Allah and say words that are appropriate."* (4:9) The meaning of the verse is that if you fear to leave your family helpless behind you, the way to protect your family is to fear Allah and the best and most durable inheritance you can provide for your children is piety.

- If you accumulate wealth because you are afraid for the future, you should rather trust Allah and believe that He is the sole Provider, Sustainer and Controller of everything. If you really trust Him, you will enjoy the feeling of tranquillity and security and hence will never worry about the future.

In addition to the points already mentioned there are four other pieces of advice to keep in mind:

- Make sure that what you earn for your living is lawful and that its source is known to be lawful.
- Exert your best efforts to acquire what is enough for you to satisfy your basic needs but do not try to obtain excessive wealth so that you do not become totally occupied and absorbed by the desire to accumulate wealth.
- Keep in mind to spend only on lawful things and do not keep your money away from required channels. You should know that spending for the Cause of Allah, whether in charity or to spread Islam, is not considered extravagance even if you were to spend all your money in that way. The verse in Qur'an that says *"Do not keep your hand chained to your neck and do not extend it to its full extent so that you sit there blamed and destitute"* (17:29) does not refer to spending for the Cause of Allah. When the Prophet, may Allah bless him and grant him peace, ordered the Muslims to spend for the sake of Allah, Abu Bakr gave him all his wealth. The Prophet asked him, "What did you leave for your children?" Abu Bakr replied, "I left for them Allah and His Messenger, and Allah will give me more" (meaning that Allah would give him more wealth in the future). 'Umar ibn al-Khattab brought half of his wealth and gave it to the Prophet, saying, "Here is half of my wealth and I should give more for the Cause of Allah."

- Make sure that your intentions are good and sincere in everything you do. In acquiring money and in spending it you should seek Allah's satisfaction. Allah says: *"Say: my prayer and my rites, my living and my dying, are for Allah alone, the Lord of all the worlds."* (6:162)

Ostentation and hypocrisy

As we have emphasised, the worth of any deed, whether it is an act of worship or not, is determined by the intention behind it. If we take for example an act which everyone does and which is not related to worship, such as eating, we will find that if we eat with the intention of keeping our body strong enough to be able to worship Allah the right way and to be a strong Muslim, following the words of the Prophet, may Allah bless him and grant him peace, "A strong believer is better than a weak believer," then the process of eating will be considered one of our good deeds. It is therefore essential to purify our intentions and make them purely for the sake of Allah in every single act we do. One piece of advice given by the Prophet stresses the desirability of hiding good deeds in order to avoid ostentation which might ruin their worth.

Abu Hurayra reports that the Prophet, may Allah bless him and grant him peace, said, "There are seven people whom Allah will shade with His shade on the Day when there is no shade but His shade: a just Imam; a youth who grows up worshipping Allah Almighty; a man whose heart is attached to the mosque; two men who love each other for the sake of Allah, meeting and parting for that reason only; a man who refuses the advances of a noble and beautiful woman, saying, 'I fear Allah'; a man who gives *sadaqa* and conceals it so that his left hand does not know what his right hand gives; and a man who remembers Allah when he is alone and his eyes overflow with tears." (*Riyad as-Salihin*, no. 376)

So we have to be careful not to spoil the purity of our intentions by ostentation or showing off, as intentions should be purely for the sake of Allah. The Prophet, may Allah bless him and grant him peace, was asked about a man who fights because of anger, a man who fights to defend himself, and a man who fights to show off, and whether any of these were in the Way of Allah. He said, "If someone fights so that the Word of Allah may be victorious, that is in the Way of Allah." (*Riyad as-Salihin*, no. 8)

Abu Hurayra related that he heard the Messenger of Allah, may Allah bless him and grant him peace, say: "The first person to be judged on the Day of Resurrection will be a man who was martyred. He will be brought and will be informed of the blessings he had and will acknowledge them. Allah will ask, 'What did you do with them?' He will reply, 'I fought for You until I was killed in battle.' Allah will say, 'You lie. Rather you fought so that it would be said, "A brave man!" And so it was said.' Then the command will be given and he will be dragged on his face until he is thrown into the Fire. There will also be a man who studied knowledge and taught it and recited the Qur'an. He will be brought and informed of his blessings, which he will acknowledge. Allah will ask, 'What did you do with them?' He will reply, 'I studied knowledge and taught it and I recited the Qur'an for You.' He will say, 'You lie. Rather you studied so that it would be said, "A scholar!" and you recited so that it would be said, "He is a reciter." And so it was said.' Then the command will be given and he will be dragged on his face until he is thrown into the Fire. There will also be a man to whom Allah gave much wealth and all kinds of property. He will be brought and informed of his blessings, which he will acknowledge. Allah will ask, 'What did you do with them?' He will reply, 'There was no cause for which You like spending to be done but that I spent in it for You.' He will say, 'You lie. Rather you did it so that it would be said, "He is generous," and so it was said.' Then the command will be given and he will be dragged on his face until he is thrown into the Fire." (*Riyad as-Salihin*, no. 1617)

The motives which lie behind apparently good deeds are frequently directed by ostentation or hypocrisy, which may be either permissible or prohibited. An example of the permissible degree of hypocrisy or ostentation is the desire to be neat and elegant in front of other people. For instance, the Prophet, may Allah bless him and grant him peace, took care to wear clean and fine clothes when meeting with delegations from the different tribes.

As regards the prohibited type of hypocrisy, one should first know that hypocrisy has three constituent factors: the deed you use as a means of showing off; the people whose satisfaction or respect you desire to gain by what you do; and the direct objective of your hypocrisy. Moreover, hypocrisy can take different forms: appearance, good deeds, words, or exploiting others.

An example of hypocrisy in appearance is growing a beard in order for people to think that you follow the *Sunna* of the Prophet, may Allah bless him and grant him peace. Hypocrisy in words involves using religious words such as *insha'llah* (if Allah wills) or *al-hamdu lillah* (praise be to Allah) or giving a religious speech at an inappropriate time, aiming only to show off. Hypocrisy in actions is to perform acts of worship, whether obligatory or voluntary ones, to show off in front of people, i.e. to display your goodness and piety to create good will among people. Hypocrisy in using others is to attempt to become close to a pious person so that people may think that you are pious as well.

If an act of worship is done out of pure hypocrisy it is not accepted. If, however, the person does an act of worship with the aim of both showing off and performing the worship, scholars differ in judging his act. Some say that the dual intentions cancel each other out while others argue, on the basis of the following *hadith qudsi,* that the act of worship is not accepted: "Allah Almighty says: 'If anyone associates something with Me, I am not affected. If anyone associates somebody with Me, I reject him and his act of associating with Me.'" (Related by Muslim) Other scholars say that reward depends on whether or not the importance of performing the worship, in the doer's sight outweighs that of showing off.

There are two types of hypocrisy in acts of worship: hypocrisy in the fundamentals of the acts of worship, and hypocrisy in the form of worship. The latter type refers to those who try to perfect their worship in front of people while they would not do so privately. As for the former type, it can be broken down into three levels:

- Hypocrisy in the foundations of religion, such as faith. *Surat al-Hujurat* refers to this category: *"The desert Arabs say, "We believe." Say: "You do not believe. Say rather, 'We have become Muslim,' for belief has not yet entered into your hearts...'"* (49:14) The punishment of such hypocrites is Hellfire according to *Surat an-Nisa'*: *"The hypocrites are in the lowest level of the Fire. You will find no helper for them."* (4:145)

- Hypocrisy in the performance of acts of worship. This is when someone believes in Islam but performs the prescribed deeds mainly to show off. This type is referred to in *Surat al-Ma'un*: *"So woe to those who pray, and are forgetful of their prayer: those who show off."* (107:4-6)

- Hypocrisy in performing voluntary acts of worship over and above the prescribed ones. By showing off in such actions a person loses the reward of doing them and commits a sin as a result of ostentation.

The most serious type of hypocrisy in actions is to pretend to be pious in order to pave the way for usurping people's rights (e.g. their money). A less serious type is to perform acts of worship in public as a means of acquiring a worldly benefit such as getting a job or getting married. A third motive could be fear of being looked down upon by people, i.e. feeling compelled to do good deeds to gain people's respect.

Ostentation and hypocrisy can be either open or hidden. Open ostentation is the kind which drives the person to do good deeds which he would not otherwise have done. Hidden ostentation, on the other hand, is hidden in the act itself. Suppose, for example, you are praying in the mosque and you feel the presence of some friends: you then feel happy that they saw you. Some scholars say that in such a situation if you turn away from that feeling immediately, you will not be judged, but if that feeling persists until the end of your prayer you might very well risk losing the entire value of your prayer. People who expect others to respect them and to be helpful to them because they observe the tenets of religion are also considered to be unwittingly ostentatious.

To deal with hypocrisy, you have to ask yourself this question before doing anything: "Am I doing it purely for the sake of Allah, or do I want people to notice it and think of me as a good Muslim?" To avoid ostentation you should always try to perform your good actions in secret – unless you sincerely aim, by making them public, to give a good example to others. When you are the imam in the prayer, do not make the prayer long, but rather keep it short. When you pray alone, make it as long as you wish. When you fast, do not go around telling people that you are fasting. The same applies to giving charity. When you are in a meeting and some question is raised and you feel you want to answer it or add to what has been said, before speaking ask yourself a question: "Why do I want to speak? Is it because I want others to see how knowledgeable I am, or is it because I really want them to share this piece of information with me?"

Therefore, the cure for hypocrisy lies in being very meticulous and serious in judging your intentions so that you make sure that whatever you do is purely for the sake of Allah alone. Allah describes those who spend in His Way seeking only His satisfaction and the reward for the sincerity of their intentions in *Surat al-Insan*:

> *"They give food, despite their love for it, to the poor and orphans and captives: 'We feed you only out of desire for the Good Pleasure of Allah. We do not want any repayment from you or any thanks. Truly We fear from our Lord a glowering, calamitous Day.' So Allah has safeguarded them from the evil of that Day and has made them meet with radiance and pure joy, and rewarded them for their steadfastness with a Garden and with silk."* (76:8-12)

Love of rank, fame and power

Desire for wealth and power are the basic components of love for this world. There is a difference between wealth and power. Love of power is more serious and dangerous because wealth requires effort to accumulate it, increase it and preserve it, while power does not require that much effort. Power leads to wealth but the reverse is not necessarily the case.

To love reputation is to love being well known and having a high position in other people's hearts so that they will obey you willingly. If your heart is overwhelmed by love of reputation, you will be preoccupied with the desire to become closer to people instead of approaching Allah. You will therefore pretend to possess qualities which make people respect you and think highly of you, and you will try to conceal the flaws in your character instead of endeavouring to cure them.

The lover of reputation often uses wrong means to achieve his goal, the most dangerous of which is to make his acts of worship known to people in order to appear as a Godfearing practising Muslim. This way the person commits the hidden sin of 'hidden idolatry' as he worships Allah in order to gain the respect of people rather than Allah's pleasure.

Every person needs friends, companions, teachers, a spouse and children. To be eager to hold a high position in the hearts of these people is a permissible love of position. A person also requires a certain standing in order to deal with people and defend himself from oppression. This type of love of standing is also permissible as long as the means to achieving it are lawful.

To protect yourself from the harmful effects of desire for position and power you should first limit your love of position to a level which is permissible. Secondly, you must make sure to reach this permissible level through legitimate means. Thirdly, you should not make show to people of good qualities which you do not possess. Fourthly, you should not seek position through making your acts of worship known to people. Fifthly, your love of standing should not be motivated by the desire to accumulate wealth. Allah says: *"That Abode of the Next World: We grant it to those who do not seek to exalt themselves in the earth..."* (28:83)

During the rule of the second Caliph, 'Umar ibn al-Khattab, whenever a group of merchants or pilgrims came from Yemen 'Umar would ask them about a man called Uways. Finally one day he met him. 'Umar asked him, "Are you Uways al-Qarani?" "Yes, Commander of the Believers," the man replied. 'Umar asked him, "Did you have leprosy, and were you cured of it except for a spot the size of a dirham?" "Yes," the man replied. 'Umar asked him, "Do you have a mother whom you treat with the utmost care and mercy?" "Yes," the man replied. 'Umar said to him, "Ask Allah to forgive me." The man was surprised and said, "Are you asking me to pray for you, Commander of the Believers? I should to ask you to pray for me." 'Umar kept repeating his request and so Uways lifted his hands and said, "May Allah forgive you, Commander of the Believers," and 'Umar repeated "Amen" after him.

Uways asked 'Umar for the reason behind all these questions. 'Umar told Uways that the Prophet, may Allah bless him and grant him peace, had once told him, "A man called Uways will come to you with the people of Yemen. He will have had leprosy and have been cured of it except for a spot the size of a dirham, and he has a mother to whom he is devoted. If you are able to request him to ask forgiveness for you, do so." 'Umar asked Uways where he was heading afterwards and Uways replied, "Syria." 'Umar asked him, "Shall I write a letter for you to its governor so that he may give you the honour which is your due?" Uways replied, "No, Commander of the Believers – I would prefer to be unknown among people." Uways then set out and no one saw him afterwards. This is the type of true standing which one should seek, one which is known by Allah and not by His servants.

Arrogance

Arrogance is to feel that your status is higher than that of other people and that you are better than they are. An arrogant man is not considered a good believer because the Prophet, may Allah bless him and grant him peace, said: "No one who has an atom's weight of pride in his heart will enter Paradise." A man said, "And if a man likes his clothes to be good and his sandals to be good?" The Prophet replied, "Allah is Beautiful and loves beauty. Pride means renouncing the truth and belittling people." (Muslim, *Riyad as-Salihin*, no. 612)

Arrogance can be inward in the sense that you are arrogant but you do not show it, meaning that it is not reflected in your actions. The reverse is outward arrogance, which does show in your behaviour as described in *Surat Luqman*: *"Do not avert your face from people out of haughtiness and do not strut about arrogantly on the earth. Allah does not love any vain or boastful person."* (31:18)

Arrogance can spring from many sources, including knowledge, beauty, good deeds, and wealth.

- A person whose arrogance is due to knowledge considers himself more knowledgeable than others and hence thinks he is closer to Allah. He expects people to acknowledge him and give him respect. The first reason for such arrogance is ignorance of what real knowledge is. The most honourable type of knowledge is knowledge of Allah and His attributes; but if you know Allah you will always remember that Pride belongs to Him alone. To know Allah you should be well aware of your real status and that you were created from earth and to earth you will return. You should remember that knowledge and understanding is a bounty from Allah. Allah says: *"We gave knowledge to Da'ud and Sulayman, who said, 'Praise be to Allah Who has favoured us over many of His believing slaves.'"* (27:15) So when Da'ud and Sulayman were given knowledge, they recognised that it was a bounty from Allah and that they owed it entirely to Allah.

    A second cause of such arrogance is when a scholar acquires knowledge before he has disciplined himself and purified his soul. Good conduct has to come before knowledge. It is related that Imam ash-Shafi'i, the founder of one of the four schools of jurisprudence, said in a poem: "I complained to Waki' (who was his teacher) about my bad memory. He advised me to keep away from sins and told me that knowledge is light and that the light of Allah is not bestowed on sinners."

    So real knowledge cannot be attained unless you first purify yourself and adhere to good conduct. If we ask ourselves the question "Who is the most knowledgeable person as far as religion is concerned?" the answer is: the Prophet, may Allah bless him and grant him peace. Yet Allah tells him in the Qur'an: *"If We willed We could take away what We have revealed to you, and then you would find no one to guard you from Us."* (17:86) This verse means that the knowledge which was given to the

Prophet, may Allah bless him and grant him peace, was from Allah, Who could take it back whenever He wished. Therefore any scholar who finds himself to be knowledgeable should always remember that this knowledge is a gift from Allah.

• Arrogance due to good deeds is when people feel superior on account of actions they perform. If you pray, fast, pay *zakat* and give charity, go on pilgrimage, and so forth, you should not feel that you are better than other people on that account, for in fact the credit for them does not in reality belong to you. Ask yourself this question: who guided you to Islam? The answer is – Allah. Who taught you how and when to pray? Allah. Who endowed you with the health, money and time to pray, pay *zakat*, and go on pilgrimage? Allah.

All your deeds are in effect bounties from Allah, so how can you feel arrogant as a result of something which is not due to you and for which you have little credit? In fact, even the process or act of thanking Allah is itself a bounty from Allah. Rabi'a al-'Adawiyya, one of the well-known religious figures, said: "Our thankfulness calls for thanks," which means that thanking Allah or feeling grateful to Him is itself a grace which requires that we thank Him again.

Anyone who thinks that he is better than other people and that others are not good Muslims will be in great trouble. The Prophet, may Allah bless him and grant him peace, said, "It is enough evil for a man that he should despise his brother Muslim." *(Riyad as-Salihin*, no. 1570; related by al-Bukhari and Muslim) Moreover, one should remember that no one enters Paradise because of his good deeds, but only by the mercy of Allah. The Prophet, may Allah bless him and grant him peace, said, "Tread the middle way and be upright but know that none of you will be saved by what he does." They asked, "Not even you, Messenger of Allah?" He said, "Not even I, unless Allah covers me with mercy and bounty from Him."

(*Riyad as-Salihin*, no. 1570; related by al-Bukhari and Muslim)

The irony is that sinners who, when they commit their sins, feel ashamed and become fearful of Allah, might on account of this fear and feeling of shame be admitted to Paradise, whereas people whose good deeds make them arrogant will find that their arrogance erases their good deeds and that they are in danger of the Fire.

- If your arrogance is based on the fact that you come from a rich and famous family, you should remember that you are judged on your own deeds alone and that you came from earth and to earth you will return, no matter who you are or who your ancestors were.

- Those whose arrogance is based on the beauty of their appearance should remember that beauty is a blessing from Allah. So if you see someone else who has less beauty than you, thank Allah for the blessing He has given you and ask Him to help you in making your conduct as good as your appearance.

- Anyone who feels arrogant because of his affluence should remember that Allah is the sole Provider of all wealth and He can withdraw it whenever He wishes. There are several examples in the Qur'an of this type of arrogance. In *Surat al-Kahf* (18:32-43), the man whom Allah provided with two gardens became arrogant and started boasting. He said to the other man: *"'I have more wealth than you, more people under me.' He entered his garden, wronging himself, and said, 'I do not think that this will ever end.'"* The other man, who was a true believer, answered him, *"Do you reject Him who created you from dust, then from a drop of sperm and then formed you as a man?"* He tried, in other words, to draw his neighbour's attention to the fact that his wealth is a blessing from Allah and that arrogance is not the proper behaviour of a believer.

What happened as a result of such arrogance? The fruits of the two gardens were ruined and the unbeliever was left wringing his hands over what he had spent on his property which had tumbled into pieces. He said, *"Oh, if only I had not associated anyone with my Lord!"* Why ddid he say this and whom had he associate with Allah? He associated himself, because he said, as is recorded in verses 35 and 36: *"I do not think that this will ever end. I do not think the Hour will ever come."*

Another Qur'anic example is the story of Qarun in *Surat al-Qasas* (28:76-82). Qarun was one of the people of Musa who managed to accumulate immense wealth by illegal means. His affluence made him an arrogant person. He said (78): *"I have only been given it because of knowledge I have."* So Qarun believed that his wealth was not from Allah but was rather due to his own merit. Those who had envied Qarun said after Allah destroyed him and his wealth (82): *"If Allah had not shown great kindness to us, we should have been swallowed up as well. Ah! Truly the rejectors are not successful."* Why would Allah cause the earth to swallow them up? What did they do? The answer is that they said (as we read in verse 79), *"Oh, if only we had the like of what Qarun has been given!"* They wished to be like Qarun; and since a person is judged by his intentions, in wanting to be like Qarun, who was an arrogant unbeliever, they thereby deserved a punishment similar to that of Qarun.

Conclusion

The heart is the repository of knowledge and true knowledge consists in knowing Allah and His attributes and learning how to reach Him and fill the heart with love of Him.

Intentions are crucial since they determine the worth of all our deeds. You might spend your life worshipping Allah but the reward of your deeds could diminish or be wiped out as a result of ostentation or arrogance. You should therefore always strive to be motivated in all your deeds by the intention of pleasing Allah. You should also avoid judging people or criticising them and instead occupy yourself with your own flaws and faults.

Remember that the Day of Judgement is *"The Day when neither wealth nor sons will be of any use – except to those who bring to Allah sound hearts."* (26:88-89) A sound heart is one which has been cured of all the illnesses discussed in this set of lessons. May Allah help us all in purifying our hearts and bestow on us His blessings and mercy so that we may be His faithful servants and receive the reward reserved for such people.

DAR AL TAQWA LTD

Publishers
Booksellers
Distributors
Printers & Stationers

BOOKS PUBLISHED BY DAR AL TAQWA LTD.

TITLE		NO.PAGES	PRICE
1. **THE MIRACLES OF THE QURAN** By Sheikh M. Al-Sharawi ISBN 1 870582 01 2	HBK PBK	276 276	£12.95 £6.50
2. **THE SIGNS BEFORE THE DAY OF JUDEGEMENT** By Ibn Kathi ISBN 1 870582 03 9	PBK	96	£3.95
3. **THE JINN IN THE QURAN AND THE SUNNA** By Mustafa Ashour ISBN 1 870582 02 0	PBK	66	£3.95
4. **THE ISRAA AND MIRAJ THE PROPHET'S NIGHT JOURNEY AND ASCENT INTO HEAVEN** By Abdul Hajjaj ISBN 1 870582 06 3	PBK	56	£3.95
5. **THE SOUL'S JOURNEY AFTER DEATH** By Layla Mabrouk ISBN 1 870582 05 5	PBK	40	£2.95
6. **YASIN AND AL-RAHMAN TRANSLATED + TRANSLITERATED** ISBN 1 870582 00 5	PBK	44	£1.50
7. **PART THIRTY OF THE HOLY QURAN ARABIC, TRANSLATED AND TRANSLITERATED** ISBN 1 870582 00 5	PBK	102	£1.95
8. **JEWELS OF GUIDANCE** By Hamza M. Salih Ajjaj ISBN 1 870582 00 4	PBK	88	£3.95
9. **THE WORLD OF THE ANGELS** By Sheikh Abdul Hamid Kishk ISBN 1 870582 00 6	PBK	96	£3.95
10. **FATE AND PREDESTINATION** By Sheikh M. Al-Sharawi ISBN 1 870582 07 1	PBK	80	£3.95
11. **DIALOGUE WITH AN ATHEIST** By Mustafa Mahmoud ISBN 1 870582 09 8 (Published May 1994)	PBK	180	£5.50

7A Melcombe Street, Baker Street, London NW16 AE
Telephone: 0171-935 6385 Facsimile: 0171-224 3894
E-mail: dar.altaqwa@btinternet.com

DAR AL TAQWA LTD

Publishers
Booksellers
Distributors
Printers & Stationers

TITLE		NO.PAGES	PRICE
12. THE INTERPRETATION OF DREAMS By Ibn Sirin ISBN 1 870582 08 X (Published May 1994)	PBK	160	£5.95
13. HOW ALLAH PROVIDES By Sheikh M. Al-Sharawi ISBN 1 870582 10 1 (Published June 1994)	PBK	96	£3.95
14. MAGIC AND ENVY By Sheikh M. Al-Sharawi ISBN 1 870582 11 X (Published July 1994)	PBK	78	£3.95
15. GOOD AND EVIL By Sheikh M. Al-Sharawi ISBN 1 870582 25 X (Published August 1994)	PBK	74	£3.95
16. THE LAWS OF MARRIAGE IN ISLAM By Sheikh M. Rif'at Uthman ISBN 1 870582 30 6 (Published March 1995)	PBK	104	£4.95
17. THE ISLAMIC WILL By Hajj Abdal Haqq + Aisha Bewley Ahmad Thomson ISBN 1 870582 35 7 (Published April 1995)	PBK	68	£5.95
18. DEALING WITH LUST AND GREED ACCORDING TO ISLAM By Sheikh 'Abdul al-Hamid Kishk ISBN 1 870582 40 3 (Published June 1995)	PBK	145	£5.95
19. TEACH YOUR CHILDREN TO LOVE OF THE PROPHET By Dr. Muhammad Abdu Yamani ISBN 1 870582 45 4 (Published June 1995)	PBK	76	£3.95
20. THE WATER OF ZAM ZAM By Muhammed Abd al Aziz Ahmad Majdi as-Sayyid Ibrahim ISBN 1 870582 55 1 (Published March 1996)	PBK	53	£3.95

7A Melcombe Street, Baker Street, London NW16 AE
Telephone: 0171-935 6385 Facsimile: 0171-224 3894
E-mail: dar.altaqwa@btinternet.com

DAR AL TAQWA LTD

**Publishers
Booksellers
Distributors
Printers & Stationers**

TITLE		NO.PAGES	PRICE
21. PORTRAIT OF HUMAN PERFECTION By Shaykh Ahmad Muhammad Al-Hawfi ISBN 1 870582 50 0 (Published March 1996)	PBK	128	£5.95
22. YAJUJ AND MAJUJ Muhyi-d-din Abd Al-Hamid ISBN 1 870582 60 8 (Published Novermber 1996)	PBK	41	£3.95
23. MUHAMMED (SAW) Dr. Mustafa Mahmoud ISBN 1 870582 70 5 (Published March 1997)	PBK	68	£3.95
24. AL MAHDI AND THE END OF TIME Muhammed ibn Izzat Muhammed Arif ISBN 1 870582 75 6 (Published May 1999)	PBK	74	£3.95
25. THE DAY OF RISING Laila Mabrouk ISBN 1 870582 85 3 (Published September 1997)	PBK	183	£5.95
26. DUNYA THE BELIEVERS PRISON, THE UNBELIVERS PARADISE Muhammad Abd Ar Rahman Iwad ISBN 1 870582 802 (Published October 1997)	PBK	160	£5.95
27. CIRCUMCISION IN ISLAM Abu Bakr Abdu'r Razzaq ISBN 1 870582 95 0 (Published August 1998)	PBK	120	£5.95
28. JOURNEY THROUGH THE QURAN THE CONTENT & CONTEXT OF THE SURAS Muhammad al-Ghazzali ISBN 1 870582 90 X (Published August 1998)	HBK	580	£25.00
29. PART 29TH OF THE QURAN ARABIC, TRANSLATED & TRANSLITERATED ISBN 1 870582 11 X (Published October 1998)	PBK	128	£2.95

7A Melcombe Street, Baker Street, London NW16 AE
Telephone: 0171-935 6385 Facsimile: 0171-224 3894
E-mail: dar.altaqwa@btinternet.com

DAR AL TAQWA LTD

Publishers
Booksellers
Distributors
Printers & Stationers

TITLE		NO.PAGES	PRICE

30. PART 28TH OF THE QURAN ARABIC, TRANSLATED & TRANSLITERATED
ISBN 1 870582 16 0
(Published October 1998)
PBK 96 £2.96

31. DIVINE EXISTENCE VERSUS DOUBT
Shaykh Muhammad M.\al-Sha'rawi
ISBN 1 87 0582 26 8
(Published February 1999)
PBK 64 £3.95

32. THE HEART & THE TONGUE
THEIR SICKNESSES AND CURES
Sheikh Yassin Roushdy
ISBN 1 870582 21 7
(Published February 1999)
PBK 48 £3.95

33. ALLAH THE DIVINE NATURE
Yassin Roushdy
ISBN 1 870582 31 4
(Published February 1999)
PBK 120 £5.95

7A Melcombe Street, Baker Street, London NW16 AE
Telephone: 0171-935 6385 Facsimile: 0171-224 3894
E-mail: dar.altaqwa@btinternet.com